The Story of America's Baseball Fields

BALLPARK

Lynn Curlee

Atheneum Books for Young Readers • New York London Toronto Sydney

Take me out to the ball game,
Take me out with the crowd.
Buy me some peanuts and Cracker Jack.
I don't care if I never get back.
Let me root, root, root for the home team,
If they don't win it's a shame.
For it's one, two, three strikes, you're out
At the old ball game.

Everyone knows the grand old song. The simple poem and jaunty tune evoke lazy, sunny summer afternoons. Fleecy clouds floating in clear blue skies. Vivid, clipped green grass and colorful advertising signs. Flags and pennants snapping in the breeze. Venders hawking hot dogs and sodas, pretzels and beer. Swelling organ music and the announcer's excited voice booming from loudspeakers. The sharp crack of bat solidly meeting ball. The deafening roar of the cheering crowd. It's a day at the ballpark!

There are thousands of baseball fields across America, ranging from schoolyard sandlots, to well-kept municipal parks with a few bleachers, to the major-league stadiums holding 50,000 fans. One of the finest is Boston's Fenway Park, a wonderful old baseball arena where even the cheapest seats are right on top of the action. Its left field is dominated by an enormous, intimidating wall—the legendary "Green Monster"—37 feet high and feared by batters for decades. Fenway has been home to the Red Sox for nearly a century, and tradition rules here—even the scoreboard is operated by hand.

Batter up at Fenway Park

Across the country Giants fans enjoy a brand-new ballpark. Beautiful SBC Park has an old-time feel, with a spectacular site on San Francisco Bay. Home runs hit over the right-field wall sometimes land right in the water, 450 feet from home plate. Barry Bonds hit fifteen of these "splash homers" in the new park's first two years.

In St. Louis, fans of the Cardinals flock to Busch Stadium, a vast, modern, circular arena capped with a ring of arches. With its rows of brilliant red seats and its huge scale, Busch Stadium was the imposing setting for Mark McGwire's home-run feats of the 1990s.

In contrast, Chicago's Wrigley Field doesn't feel imposing at all. Almost as old as Fenway, the home of the Cubs is friendly and intimate, with only a low brick wall to separate the sweeping grandstand from the playing field. The wall continues right around the outfield, but it is higher there and completely covered with thick, dark green ivy. People in buildings across the street can see right into the park. On a glorious summer day, during an exciting game, in the midst of a cheering crowd with the scoreboard pennants waving in the breezes from Lake Michigan, Wrigley Field is considered by Cubs fans the most beautiful and perfect ballpark of all.

If it seems baseball fans feel passionate about their parks, well, they are, for good reason. While most team sports are played on a rectangular field, with a goal for each team at the ends, a baseball playing field has a wedge layout, with a diamond-shaped infield in one corner, surrounded on two sides by an enormous outfield. Every football gridiron is exactly the same size. Every basketball court is identical. But beyond the infield diamond, every baseball park is unique. The shape and size of the outfield; the height and position of fences, walls, flagpoles, scoreboards, and other obstacles; the configuration of the grandstand with its decks and roofs; the amount of wind; even the altitude above sea level—all can affect the play of the game.

New ballparks have been built by each generation, and old ones have been destroyed or replaced as times have changed. Some ballparks are better than others. The best baseball parks acquire an aura. These are the places dedicated to the rituals of the game, where the heroes of the past performed their miracles and where the players of today may perform theirs. For many fans the great ballparks are like shrines—America's "green cathedrals."

DIAGRAM OF A BASEBALL FIELD

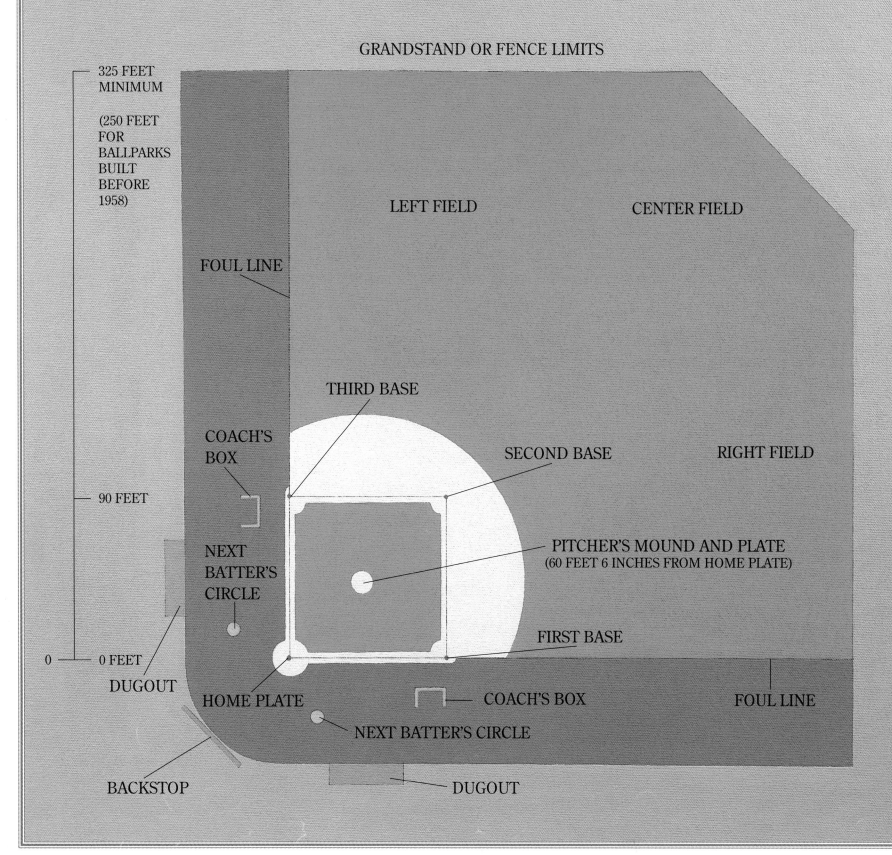

GRANDSTAND OR FENCE LIMITS

325 FEET
MINIMUM

(250 FEET
FOR
BALLPARKS
BUILT
BEFORE
1958)

LEFT FIELD

CENTER FIELD

FOUL LINE

THIRD BASE

COACH'S
BOX

SECOND BASE

RIGHT FIELD

90 FEET

NEXT
BATTER'S
CIRCLE

PITCHER'S MOUND AND PLATE
(60 FEET 6 INCHES FROM HOME PLATE)

0   0 FEET

FIRST BASE

DUGOUT

HOME PLATE

COACH'S BOX

FOUL LINE

NEXT BATTER'S CIRCLE

BACKSTOP

DUGOUT

Baseball is one of the great American traditions. Professional football and basket-ball came into their own more recently and now are just as popular, but for a long time baseball was the sport that mattered most, and maybe it still does. Since the Civil War era, baseball has been called our "national pastime." Before computers or television or radio, before movies or airplanes or automobiles, even before electricity, there was baseball. The history of the sport reflects the story of our country, the changes in our society over the decades, and even something of our national character. As the great American poet Walt Whitman said, baseball has the "snap, go, fling of the American atmosphere. . . . It's our game."

Bat-and-ball games were common in early America. There is an account of soldiers "playing at base" at Valley Forge, and newspapers record games of "base ball" as early as 1823. By the mid-nineteenth century young professional gentlemen in New York, Boston, and Philadelphia were joining social clubs that competed in ball games.

Our modern game of baseball was born in New York City in 1845. A twenty-five-year-old clerk named Alexander J. Cartwright organized a group of his friends as the Knickerbocker Base Ball Club. Taking elements from older games, the young men developed a set of written rules, many of which still stand today. On June 19, 1846, the Knickerbockers played their first official match against the New York Base Ball Club, also known as the "New York Nine." Although they had practiced in Manhattan at places like Madison Square Park, this first real game was held on a grassy lot poeti-cally called the "Elysian Fields" in a park overlooking the Hudson River in Hoboken, New Jersey, a short ferry ride from the players' homes in New York. Cartwright served as umpire, and the Knickerbockers lost.

But their rules were not lost. They gave the game its nine-inning structure and determined the number of players and their positions as well as the layout of the diamond. But the most important

Baseball in the 1850s

4

innovation was this: In earlier games a player running bases could be put out by being hit by a thrown ball. Now he could be put out only at base or by being tagged by another player holding the ball. As a result, a smaller, harder, more lively ball could be used. This made for a faster, more rugged and exciting contest, and enthusiasm for the Knickerbocker form of the game spread. Gradually, over the next decade, as the new rules were adopted all over the Northeast, games between the various clubs started drawing audiences, and baseball became a spectator sport. In 1858, for the first time, 4,000 gentlemen in top hats and ladies in hoop skirts actually paid admission to see a match between New York and Brooklyn all-star teams at the Fashion Race Course, a horse-racing arena on Long Island.

But it was during the Civil War that baseball really took root. Soldiers who knew the game taught it to their platoons, prisoners taught it to their guards, and the game of baseball spread throughout both armies. Requiring nothing more than a flat open space, a ball, and a bat, pickup games were played whenever soldiers had some free time. And after the war was over, the soldiers took baseball home with them, to every part of America.

The Knickerbockers had been young professional gentlemen, out for a day of sport. After the Civil War, baseball was embraced as a serious enterprise by working-class immigrants from Europe who were filling the big cities and by farm boys in small towns all over the country. Baseball clubs sprang up everywhere. Some clubs even began paying their best players. In 1869 the first true professional baseball team was organized—the Cincinnati Red Stockings. Playing baseball was their job, and they toured from New York to San Francisco that year playing against amateur clubs all over the country. They won more than fifty games and tied one. This prompted other clubs to hire young men to play ball, and the game of baseball became a business.

Since one of the main goals of a business is to make money, clubs began to charge fans a fee to see their games. In the summer of 1862, during the Civil War, an enterprising fellow named William Cammeyer drained the large ice-skating arena that he owned in Brooklyn and opened it for baseball. He provided a small grandstand for seating the ladies, and he charged admission. It was called Union Grounds. With the rise of professional ball, club owners began enclosing their own baseball fields and building grandstands for the paying customers. The baseball park was born.

Union soldiers at play during the Civil War

During the late nineteenth century, an era known as the Gilded Age, the business of baseball boomed, and dozens of professional teams were organized. As the game became ever more popular the ballparks were made larger and grander. By the mid-1880s extravagant wooden "baseball palaces" were drawing thousands of fans. Boston's Grand Pavilion, home of the Beaneaters, was one of the first double-decker arenas. It was capped with an ornate turreted roof to shade the crowd. At St. George Grounds in Staten Island, New York, baseball wasn't the only entertainment. There were also marching bands, fountains, tennis courts, and restaurants. But one of the most elaborate of the Gilded Age parks was the Palace of the Fans, built in Cincinnati just after the turn of the century. Made to resemble a Roman temple, the grandstand was decorated with columns and featured exclusive "fashion boxes" for wealthier patrons—the predecessor of our "box seats."

Along with the ballparks, the game itself was changing. Play became rougher and faster. A new generation of ballplayers tested the limits of the rules, introducing radical practices like the curveball, bunting, base stealing, and sliding, which are now standard. As the game became less genteel and more physical, gloves, catcher's masks, and padding were introduced for protection. Popular players, such as Al Spalding, Cap Anson, and Mike "King" Kelly, captured the public imagination, and they became the first baseball stars. Gradually, the most important professional teams from the large eastern cities were organized into two major leagues, each with eight teams. In 1903 the National League and the American League established a National Commission run by the owners to govern the sport, and the first World Series was held. By the beginning of the twentieth century America's national pastime had become an institution.

The big baseball palaces of the Gilded Age, although impressive, had one major flaw. Because they were made of wood, they were dangerously flammable. In 1894 alone, four major ballparks burned down. Boston's Grand Pavilion was set ablaze during a game when a group of children set fire to some debris under the bleachers. Over the years scores of people were injured in ballpark fires. But it was not until 1909 that a relatively safe and fireproof ballpark was built. Shibe Park in Philadelphia was the first park to be made of steel and concrete. While in keeping with the grand tradition of its predecessors, with its ornate brick facade and distinctive corner tower, Shibe was not only

Boston's Grand Pavilion

much safer than the wooden parks, it was also much larger. In addition to the playing field and grandstand, it contained the team's offices, locker rooms, and pressrooms, and the first real dugouts. It was solid and permanent, and when it was first built, could hold a crowd of 20,000 fans. Shibe Park was the wave of the future.

Clubs in other cities quickly followed suit, and within five years, most of the legendary classic ballparks of the early twentieth century were constructed: Forbes Field in Pittsburgh, Chicago's Comiskey Park, Griffith Stadium in Washington, D.C., the Polo Grounds in New York, Boston's Fenway Park, Crosley Field in Cincinnati, Tiger Stadium in Detroit, Brooklyn's Ebbets Field, Braves Field in Boston, and Wrigley Field in Chicago. The smallest (Ebbets and Wrigley) could hold 18,000 fans originally, while the largest (Braves) had a capacity of 40,000. Their scale was perfect for watching baseball. Wrigley Field, Fenway Park, and Ebbets Field, in particular, were referred to as urban "jewel boxes"—cozy and intimate places where the fans felt part of the game.

Besides being constructed of steel and concrete, these parks had something else in common. At a time when very few people had automobiles, fans had to be able to get to the ball game easily, whether by trolley or streetcar, or in later years, by train or bus. Therefore, the parks were located near urban centers with access to public transportation lines. While Griffith Stadium, the Polo Grounds, and Crosley Field were built to replace burned wooden parks, others, like Fenway Park and Ebbets Field, were newly shoehorned into existing neighborhoods so that the location of streets and other buildings determined the size and shape of the outfield and grandstands. So each ballpark was unique, with its own quirks, advantages, and disadvantages.

As for the sport itself, in an era before power hitters, the early-twentieth-century game was dominated by great pitchers. Men like Cy Young, Walter Johnson, and Christy Mathewson ruled from the mound. But the greatest player of the time was a versatile, all-around athlete from Georgia named Ty Cobb. He spent most of his legendary career with the Detroit Tigers, where he perfected a close infield game of precision hits and runs—a game of strategy. Fast, aggressive, and intimidating, Cobb played a kind of "slash-and-burn" baseball. He is still considered one of the most important and influential players of all time.

DIAGRAM OF FENWAY PARK

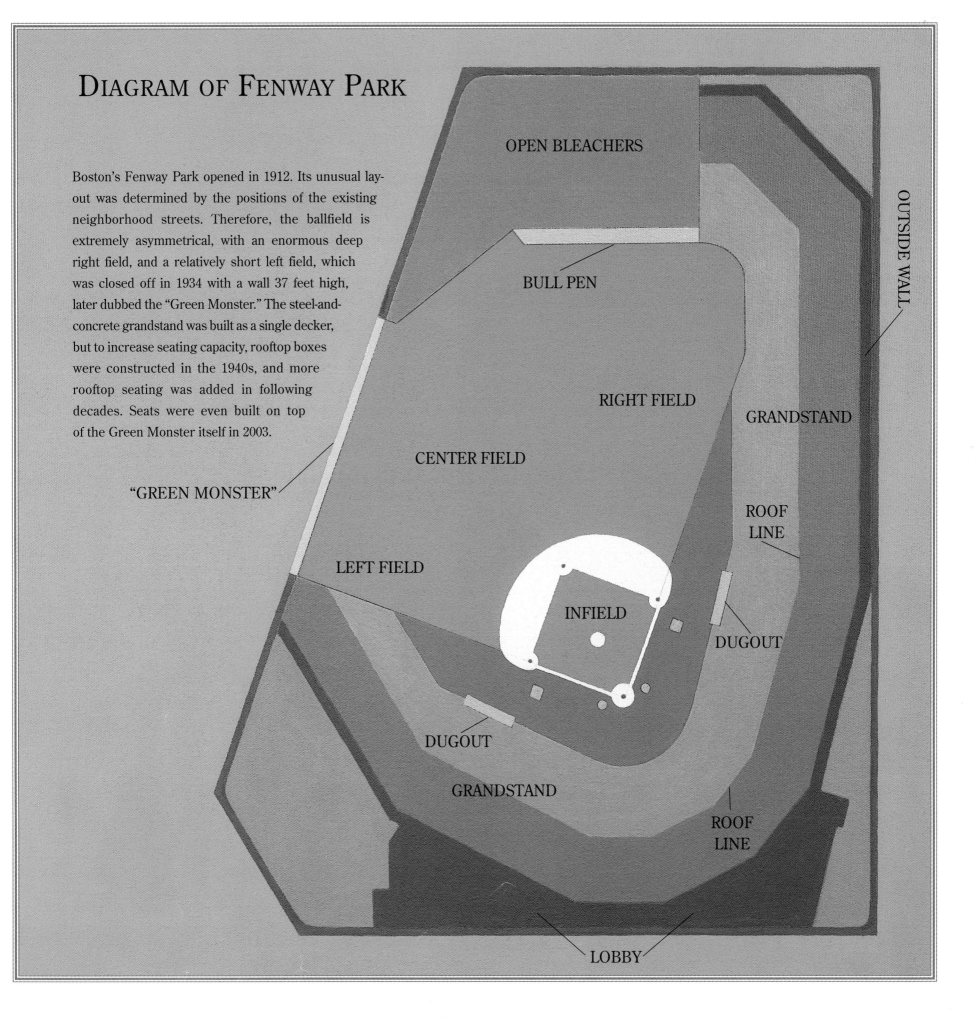

Boston's Fenway Park opened in 1912. Its unusual layout was determined by the positions of the existing neighborhood streets. Therefore, the ballfield is extremely asymmetrical, with an enormous deep right field, and a relatively short left field, which was closed off in 1934 with a wall 37 feet high, later dubbed the "Green Monster." The steel-and-concrete grandstand was built as a single decker, but to increase seating capacity, rooftop boxes were constructed in the 1940s, and more rooftop seating was added in following decades. Seats were even built on top of the Green Monster itself in 2003.

OPEN BLEACHERS

OUTSIDE WALL

BULL PEN

RIGHT FIELD

GRANDSTAND

CENTER FIELD

ROOF LINE

"GREEN MONSTER"

LEFT FIELD

INFIELD

DUGOUT

DUGOUT

GRANDSTAND

ROOF LINE

LOBBY

As the baseball boom continued during the early twentieth century, even the president of the United States got involved. On April 14, 1910, William Howard Taft, our twenty-seventh president, threw the first ball of the season onto the field at National Park in Washington, D.C. (A wooden park, National would burn down the next year, to be replaced by a steel-and-concrete structure, later named Griffith Stadium.) President Taft had played ball in his youth; he loved the game and wanted to associate himself with the national pastime. This began a ritual, which continues today. Nearly every president since Taft has thrown out the first ball to start the baseball season from the nation's capital.

It was seven years later, in 1917, that America entered World War I. And one of the grandest traditions in all of sports was begun in wartime during the first game of the 1918 World Series at Comiskey Park, between the Chicago Cubs and the Boston Red Sox. According to a newspaper account, during the regular break in the game called the "seventh-inning stretch," as the crowd got up and started moving around, "the band broke forth to the strains of 'The Star-Spangled Banner.' . . . Heads were bared as the ball players turned quickly about and faced the music. . . . First the song was taken up by a few, then others joined, and when the final notes came, a great volume of melody rolled across the field. It was at the very end that the onlookers exploded into thunderous applause and rent the air with a cheer." People were so touched that this event was repeated at every game of the series. Thirteen years before being officially named the national anthem, the stirring, patriotic song became part of baseball tradition, and it has been performed at the beginning of every game for more than sixty years.

Previous page: The legendary Ty Cobb (sliding) was known for his aggressive style of play. Opposite: President Taft throws out the first ball in 1910.

World War I ended on November 11, 1918, and the world of professional baseball was rocked by the worst scandal in its history the very next year. The World Series of 1919, a contest between the Chicago White Sox and the Cincinnati Reds, was fixed. Eight Chicago players, including star hitter "Shoeless" Joe Jackson, conspired with professional gamblers to deliberately lose the game. Earlier, the White Sox had nicknamed themselves the "Black Sox" because their owner was too cheap to pay for laundering their uniforms, and the name stuck to the incident. The Black Sox scandal threatened to harm the business of baseball, so to preserve the integrity of the game, the old National Commission run by the owners was dissolved and an independent Commissioner of Baseball was named to govern the sport. Although they had been exploited by professional gamblers and were acquitted in court, the players were harshly punished. The new commissioner banned them from baseball for life. The infamous Black Sox scandal of 1919 alienated many fans, but their faith was to be restored very soon.

His name was George Herman Ruth, but he was known as the "Babe," and he would change baseball forever. He had a hard childhood and sadly felt that his parents never loved him. As he grew older and wilder, he became difficult to handle, and his parents packed him off to reform school. There he found an encouraging mentor and a refuge in baseball. He was a natural, and he channeled his energy into the game. As he grew up, talent scouts quickly noticed his ability, and at the age of nineteen he was hired by the Boston Red Sox as a pitcher. He was a great one. He was a great player at *any* position, but with a bat in his hands, he was the greatest. In 1919, his sixth season, he slammed a record 29 home runs. Before the Babe, home runs were uncommon, almost accidental events. The previous record was 27 home runs, set 35 years earlier in 1884, when ballparks were generally smaller.

Babe Ruth, the Sultan of Swat

The very next year Babe Ruth was sold to the New York Yankees for the astonishing sum of $125,000. It turned out to be quite a bargain for the Yankees. Ruth slammed an amazing 54 home runs that year, almost doubling his own record, a feat many consider his greatest achievement. Only one other entire *team* hit as many! In 1921 the figure jumped to 59. The fans adored him. Kids worshipped him. He was larger than life, he sizzled with charisma, and he loved playing for his audience. Fans flocked to the ballpark to see him play.

The Yankees played at the Polo Grounds, owned by the New York Giants. Jealous of Babe Ruth's crowd appeal, the Giants refused to renew the rival team's lease, so the Yankees' management decided to build a new ballpark of their own to showcase their star. They chose a site in the Bronx, almost directly across the Harlem River from the Polo Grounds. The new ballpark was the superstadium of its era. Nicknamed "the House That Ruth Built," Yankee Stadium had the first triple-deck grandstand and could hold 58,000 fans. The immense grandstand curved majestically around the infield, and its roof was capped by an ornamental scalloped copper frieze. It had a vast and solid grandeur unlike any other ballpark.

April 18, 1923, was opening day at Yankee Stadium, and the Babe delivered the goods. According to the *New York Times,* as the "Sultan of Swat" smashed a savage home run the tremendous crowd "rose to its feet and let loose the biggest shout in baseball history." For the rest of the twentieth century the Yankees would be the "winningest" team in baseball, and Yankee Stadium became the most famous athletic arena in the world—it has even been called the "Temple of Sport."

Yankee Stadium's triple-deck grandstand curves majestically around the infield.

It was the Roaring Twenties, the Jazz Age, and it was the beginning of the game's "Golden Era." Movies—an amazing new kind of entertainment—were the latest rage, and for the first time baseball fans could see newsreels of their heroes in action. Major-league games were no longer local events; now they made national news. In 1927 Babe Ruth hit 60 home runs—setting perhaps the most famous record in sports history. As he approached the record game by game, the nation was galvanized by the countdown. Everyone followed it in newspapers, watched it in newsreels, and heard about it on their newfangled radios. Babe Ruth was the first superstar of sports. A baseball player had actually become the most famous man in America!

The first commercial radio station had gone on the air in 1920. From the beginning, World Series games were broadcast locally, then local stations began carrying regular-season games. By the 1930s national radio networks were bringing major-league baseball live over the airwaves to all of America. Baseball and radio were a perfect match. With the sounds of the organ music and the reactions of the crowd in the background, a gifted sportscaster could make a ballpark come vividly alive in a listener's mind as he dramatically described the play-by-play. After the crash of the stock market in 1929 the nation slid into the Great Depression. Baseball on the radio was wonderful free entertainment in hard times, and more people became baseball fans than ever before by listening to games.

People could also watch live professional baseball in many smaller cities and towns. The big leagues began using minor-league ball clubs all over the country as "farms" for talent. And then there were the African-American ball clubs, known collectively as the "Negro Leagues." During this era American society was almost totally segregated in a way that is practically impossible to imagine today. For decades the major leagues had strictly enforced an unspoken rule: There would be no mixing of the races in professional baseball. As a result, an entire parallel world of black baseball

Baseball in small-town America, 1930s

had flourished. The Negro Leagues had their own organization, their own teams, their own stars, and their own audience. Men like Josh Gibson and Leroy "Satchel" Paige were among the greatest of all baseball players, but they were almost unknown among most major-league fans at the time.

The minor leagues and the Negro Leagues played in every kind of ballpark imaginable. Some teams had their own small ballparks, while others toured around the country—from local town lots with a few bleachers to municipal stadiums to the major-league arenas, which were rented out when the big clubs were out of town.

Night baseball was another important innovation. Beginning in 1929 floodlights were used to illuminate ballparks for night games, first in the Negro Leagues, then in the minors. The first major-league game under the lights took place at Crosley Field in Cincinnati in 1935. The momentous occasion was marked by a ceremony before the game began. The curious crowd arrived at dusk to see a large lightbulb mounted on a table on the ball field. During the twilight ceremony President Franklin D. Roosevelt, linked by telephone, threw a switch in the White House, hundreds of miles away. The bulb suddenly blazed into light, and at this signal, the ballpark lights on their tall spindly poles were turned on. The crowd cheered as Crosley Field was bathed in an electric glow. Not everyone, however, welcomed night games. Baseball purists were appalled. But gradually, almost all of the major-league parks installed lights. All except one. As a defiant gesture in favor of tradition, the Chicago Cubs held out for half a century. Wrigley Field had no lights until 1988!

The late '30s saw the end of some legendary careers. Babe Ruth hit his final home run in 1935 for an unparalleled career total of 714. His teammate Lou Gehrig, the Yankees' "Iron Horse," played in an amazing 2,130 consecutive games before he was forced to retire when diagnosed with a fatal illness. At the time it truly seemed as though these records could never be broken. Baseball's most intensely moving moment took place in Yankee Stadium on July 4, 1939, when Gehrig was honored for his contributions to the game. In the face of a tragic early death he saluted his family, teammates, and fans with the most famous speech in baseball history. His words echoed throughout the vast arena: "Today I consider myself the luckiest man on the face of the earth." The Baseball Hall of Fame was also founded in 1939. The first group of inductees included Babe Ruth, of course, but the man who received the most votes was Ty Cobb.

The first major-league night game was held at Crosley Field.

As the old guard left the game a new generation of exciting players was emerging: men like Boston slugger Ted Williams and "Joltin'" Joe DiMaggio, the Yankee Clipper who took Ruth's place as the star of the Yankee lineup. But their dazzling careers were interrupted by world events. On December 7, 1941, the Japanese bombed Pearl Harbor, and the United States entered World War II. President Roosevelt, a longtime baseball fan, wrote a letter to the Commissioner of Baseball, urging that the game continue during wartime. He considered baseball crucial to the morale of the nation. At the same time, however, individual players were citizens who were expected to serve their country. During the course of the war 340 major leaguers went into the armed forces, including DiMaggio and Williams, who distinguished himself as a marine pilot. Their places in the club rosters were taken by older men or others ineligible to serve. The St. Louis Browns actually had an outfielder, Pete Gray, with only one arm! Gray proved himself to be a surprisingly good fielder. Games became patriotic events, and baseball was valued more than ever as the great American game with a central position at the very heart of our nation's culture.

When the war was over, baseball confronted the worst of America—the festering issue of race. After DiMaggio and Williams and all the other war veterans returned to the game in 1946, it seemed as though things would return to the way they had always been. But one of the club owners decided the time was right for a change. Branch Rickey of the Brooklyn Dodgers courageously defied the unspoken rule and hired an African American to play major-league baseball. Jackie Robinson was a military veteran and a superb all-around athlete. Handsome, with immense personal dignity and charisma, he had a scrappy, daring style of play. Rickey felt that Robinson would be a great asset to the club, and he was right.

Ebbets Field was filled to capacity on April 15, 1947, when Jackie Robinson first took the field and made history. He was chosen not only for his athletic ability, but also because he had the strength of character to face whatever insults were hurled his way and give back great baseball. And incidentally, whenever he played, the ballpark was packed. The color barrier was broken in baseball 15 years before the civil rights movement of the 1960s. It has been called baseball's finest hour.

Bomber over the Bronx—baseball continued to be played during World War II.

It would take several years, but Jackie Robinson opened the door for future stars like Willie Mays, Hank Aaron, and Roberto Clemente, the first Latino player. But ironically, breaking the color barrier also meant the end of Negro League baseball, with its own rich heritage as a proud and central part of the African-American community.

America, too, was changing at midcentury. Veterans of the war were raising families and moving to the suburbs. Everyone was buying a new car and the latest invention, a television. From the beginning baseball was a main event on TV. After years of only hearing games on the radio, fans could now actually see major-league baseball from their homes. At first, club owners were wary of the new medium, fearing that people would stay away from the ballparks, but soon advertising dollars were making them wealthy beyond their dreams.

During the 1950s, New York City was the "capital of baseball." It boasted three great teams whose rivalry dominated the game, and it was also the center of TV broadcasting. Each team had its own ballpark. The "Bronx Bombers," the Yankees, played in the classiest, most dignified ballpark of all, Yankee Stadium. The venerable New York Giants owned the Polo Grounds in Manhattan, the third park since the 1880s to be built on the same site. The last one had burned down in 1911. Shaped like a gigantic bathtub, the Polo Grounds' unusual grandstand was tucked under a cliff called "Coogan's Bluff," where fans could gather and look down on games for free. And the Brooklyn Dodgers' home was Ebbets Field, built on the site of a garbage dump once called "Pigtown." It was a utilitarian, blue-collar sort of ballpark, but it had a grand entrance. The lobby rotunda had a marble floor with inlaid baseball stitches and a huge chandelier in the form of bats and balls.

This was the era of young Mickey Mantle, Yogi Berra, Willie Mays, and Duke Snider. Thanks to television, fans all over the country had their own favorite New York team and rooted for individual stars. In 1955 they watched the Brooklyn Dodgers take the National League pennant and then go on to beat their archrival, the Yankees, and win the World Series. Known to their fans as "Dem Bums," the Dodgers had been underdogs for four decades, but now they were a great team, and their fans

Previous page: The color barrier in baseball was broken by Jackie Robinson.
Opposite: Ebbets Field—game day

were among the most fiercely loyal in all of baseball. The Dodgers had come to represent the heart and soul of Brooklyn, and the championship was the sweetest of victories.

The very next year the Dodgers once again faced the Yankees in the fall classic. This time the Yankees took it, but Brooklyn battled it out for seven games. This series is particularly famous for its fifth game. Yankee pitcher Don Larsen achieved something never done in a World Series before or since. It was that rarest of baseball events, a perfect game, in which a pitcher allows no batter to safely reach first base. And television brought all of this excitement from the ballpark directly into America's living rooms. Baseball in the prosperous mid-'50s basked in its popularity and in its position as a great American institution.

But a big change was in the air. First the Boston Braves moved to Milwaukee in 1953. Then the St. Louis Browns transferred to Baltimore and became the Orioles, and the Philadelphia Athletics went to Kansas City. These were all lesser teams in the majors, but then the nearly unthinkable happened. In 1957 the owners of both the New York Giants and the Brooklyn Dodgers decided to move their clubs to the West Coast. They became the San Francisco Giants and the Los Angeles Dodgers. Moving west was very smart business. Until now major-league baseball was limited to the urban Northeast, while the population of America was moving west and south. But for two generations, in spite of depression and war, baseball had been nearly constant; teams didn't move around. A major-league baseball team was part of the identity of a city. And for fans, particularly Brooklyn fans, the move felt like the ultimate betrayal.

Soon afterward, Ebbets Field was the scene of a small ceremony on February 23, 1960. The national anthem was sung, a brass band played "Auld Lang Syne," then the wrecking ball began its work. The famous old ballpark was razed to make room for apartment buildings. Four years later the Polo Grounds was demolished with the exact same two-ton wrecking ball. The ball was painted to resemble a baseball. The game's Golden Era was over.

"Auld Lang Syne"—Ebbets Field under the wrecking ball

In 1961 Yankee Roger Maris blasted 61 home runs, breaking Babe Ruth's single season record. Maris was quiet, shy, and uncomfortable with stardom, and many fans seemed almost to resent his achievement. By now Babe Ruth had passed beyond legend to become one of the all-time great American icons. The broken record was another symbol of the changing game.

By the early '60s, the Giants and the Dodgers had settled into brand-new baseball parks in California. From the beginning, Candlestick Park in San Francisco, with chilly, unpredictable weather and strong winds, was disliked by many fans and players alike. It has been said that Willie Mays, who many people consider the greatest player of all time, was robbed of his ultimate rightful place in the record book as the home-run king by the winds in Candlestick Park. On the other hand, Dodger Stadium in Los Angeles was a huge success. Fans could thrill to the amazing talent of pitcher Sandy Koufax while basking in the southern California sunshine and enjoying the beautiful view of the distant mountains. Considered the best of the midcentury parks, Dodger Stadium is an exquisitely maintained arena that sits in the middle of a vast parking lot. Until the '60s most major-league parks had been embedded in big-city neighborhoods with good public transportation. Now that everyone had cars, ballparks could be located anywhere near population centers. Cities all over the country began exploring the idea of attracting a major-league baseball club. And, subsequently, in the early 1960s the business of baseball expanded by authorizing new teams.

The California Angels was the first brand-new club since the early twentieth century. Then the New York Mets opened for business, followed by the Houston Astros. By the end of the '60s, seven new "expansion teams" had joined the ranks of major-league baseball, and a new generation of ballparks was being constructed. At first the new clubs played in older ballparks. The Angels had played in a minor-league park until their own ballpark was built in Anaheim in 1966, and the Mets had played at the aging Polo Grounds, abandoned by the Giants, until Shea Stadium was built in Queens. Finished in 1964,

Dodger Stadium in Los Angeles

Shea is a saucer-shaped stadium, open at center field and surrounded by a huge parking lot. It was among the very first of its type.

The most radical new stadium was the Houston Astrodome, opened in 1965. Billed as the "Eighth Wonder of the World," it was a totally enclosed circular arena seating 42,000 under an immense shallow dome 18 stories high. The Astrodome was a ballpark for the space age, but it had some kinks. Players complained that they couldn't see fly balls against the translucent ceiling. When the roof was painted to solve the problem, the grass died from lack of light. The answer to that was AstroTurf, perhaps the most controversial innovation in baseball history. One player quipped, "If the horses won't eat it, I won't play on it." But by the 1980s more than half of major-league games were played on AstroTurf. It was simply less expensive to maintain than natural grass.

In 1969 the New York Mets were the first expansion team to win the World Series. The Brooklyn Dodgers could never be replaced in the hearts of New Yorkers, but the underdog "Miracle Mets" of 1969 came close. It was truly a new era. And the changing business of baseball was about to be rocked once more. The Major League Baseball Players Association walked out on strike on opening day of the 1972 season. This had never happened before, and it was a shock to fans and club owners alike. Under the old system, a player was bound to a particular club for his entire career, unless traded or sold or fired. Now the players wanted free agency—to be able to sell their services to the highest bidder. By the early 1980s stars were negotiating million-dollar contracts and even average players were very well paid.

Baseball had become very big business indeed, and the ballpark building boom lasted throughout the 1960s and 1970s as the expansion continued. Many of the aging classic ballparks were retired. Now considered obsolete, Crosley Field, Griffith Stadium, Forbes Field, and Shibe Park were demolished in favor of the new style "concrete doughnuts" in Cincinnati, Washington, D.C., Pittsburgh, and Philadelphia. Cavernous, circular arenas, which were used for other sports besides baseball, were also built in St. Louis, Atlanta, San Diego, and other cities. Although their capacity was about the same as that of Yankee Stadium, the new circular shape made them seem much larger and caused fans to be seated farther from the action. These superstadiums were immense,

The Cardinals at practice in Busch Stadium

luxurious, and impressive architecturally, with multiple concession areas, escalators for ease of access, deluxe private boxes for corporate sponsors or wealthy patrons, and elaborate electronic scoreboards. But many fans considered them to be impersonal and bland, without the intimate scale, asymmetry, and unusual quirks that made the old ballparks so beloved. "I stand at the plate," complained one player, "and I honestly don't know whether I'm in Pittsburgh, Cincinnati, St. Louis, or Philly. They all look alike." Even Yankee Stadium itself got a makeover in 1974–75 that made it more modern and efficient, with a rebuilt upper deck, expanded concession areas, escalators, and luxury boxes. But inevitably, some of its character was stripped away. The famous trademark scalloped copper frieze was even removed from the grandstand roof and a copy installed atop the outfield fence.

But the game never failed to provide thrilling moments. In 1974, during the Braves' home opener in Atlanta, slugger Hank Aaron broke Babe Ruth's long-standing career record of 714 home runs with number 715. A veteran of 20 years with the Braves, Aaron was the last great player who had begun his career in the Negro Leagues. He would go on to score a career total of 755 home runs.

The 1980s began with another players' strike. This time players were out for 50 days at the height of the '81 season, and more than 700 games were cancelled. The legal battle over the details of free agency at first bored and then infuriated the fans. They just wanted to see great baseball. But the business of baseball had to change with the times, and so did the ballparks. The cookie-cutter, saucer-shaped stadiums of the '60s and '70s saw a lot of exciting games, but the arenas themselves were not loved like the old classic urban ballparks. They might be efficient and luxurious, and perfect for football, but huge superstadiums laid with AstroTurf weren't what people thought of as baseball parks. And in the 1990s there was a backlash.

Ballpark designers began studying the old parks to try to recapture what made them so special. The Orioles opened their 1992 season in a brand-new ballpark in downtown Baltimore. Oriole Park at Camden Yards has the intimate feeling of a classic urban ballpark like Wrigley Field or Fenway Park. The grandstand wraps asymmetrically around the diamond, and an enormous restored old warehouse from the early twentieth century closes off right field. There is no AstroTurf here; instead there's a scrupulously manicured carpet of grass. At the same time, it is a state-of-the-art facility, with an enormous

Hank Aaron holds the lifetime home-run record.

video-display electronic scoreboard, wonderful restaurants, and every amenity. What's more, it is actually built on the site where Babe Ruth's father owned a bar. Talk about history! Camden Yards blends beautifully into the old waterfront neighborhood. It was an instant classic. The fans loved it, the players loved it, and clubs all over the country suddenly wanted a retro park of their own.

By 2000 many new major-league ballparks were in operation, with more under construction or being planned. The new baseball-only parks in such cities as Denver, Cleveland, Detroit, Atlanta, Houston, and San Francisco have followed the lead of Camden Yards, offering the fans all they have come to expect at a modern sports arena but simultaneously serving up a nostalgic baseball experience. Some of these ballparks have amazing retracting roofs, others have museum exhibits or amusement rides or lavish restaurants, but they are all real baseball parks.

Best of all, the game itself seems to have entered a new phase. Players may now be multimillionaires, but the new generation is also bigger, stronger, faster, and better conditioned than ever before. On September 6, 1995, the president and vice president of the United States were in the grandstand at Camden Yards with 46,000 other fans to see "Iron Man" Cal Ripken Jr. make history as he played in his 2,131st consecutive game. Lou Gehrig's fifty-six-year-old record was broken, and Ripken went on to number 2,632 before his streak ended.

Then, in 1998, the season home-run record was once more under siege. As the season progressed Cardinal Mark McGwire and Sammy Sosa of the Cubs both closed in on the record, and once again the entire nation followed the countdown. On September 8, during a Cardinals/Cubs game at Busch Stadium, McGwire blasted number 62 and became the new home-run king. He was embraced by Sosa after rounding the bases. Roger Maris's record had stood for 37 years, three years longer than Babe Ruth's. McGwire finished the season with 70 home runs, with Sosa close behind at 66. This time fans were not ambivalent. They rejoiced. The record was not just broken, it had been totally shattered. Then, in 2001, it happened again when Barry Bonds of the Giants made it to number 73. It is a new era in the game, and ballparks are packed once more.

Sadly, only two of the classic pre–World War I ballparks remain. Beautiful Wrigley Field in Chicago has its ivy-covered outfield wall and its reputation as the last holdout against night games.

"Iron Man" Cal Ripken played in more consecutive games than any other player.

Here legend says that Babe Ruth called a shot during the 1932 World Series when he pointed toward the outfield and then put the ball over the fence. Boston's Fenway Park has its Green Monster, still the most infamous physical and psychological barrier in baseball. Home of Ted Williams's amazing career, Fenway is the oldest ballpark currently in operation and seems almost suspended in time. Red Sox fans take their baseball very seriously, and Fenway is their shrine. It is one of the most beloved of the "green cathedrals."

America's "game of summer" was enjoyed by our grandparents, and it will be enjoyed by our grandchildren. Baseball links us with our past and our future. Now in the twenty-first century there is a new spirit in the air, with a new generation of players, a new generation of fans, and a new generation of ballparks to take their places beside the old. The national pastime looks ahead. Let the game continue.

Play ball!

Opposite: Wrigley Field—one of the original "green cathedrals"
Following page: Play ball!

In loving memory of my niece, Ann Davis Brown,

and for Sherry and Charles, Jim and Kay, and all the kids

NOTE

There are many, many astonishing feats, records broken, and compelling stories
about ballplayers that could not be included in a mere forty-eight pages. My hope
is that in this celebration of ballparks, I'll have whetted your appetite to learn more
about the parks, the players, and the glorious game of baseball.

Bibliography

Astor, Gerald and the National Baseball Hall of Fame. *The Baseball Hall of Fame 50th Anniversary Book.* New York: Prentice Hall Press, 1998.

Baseball As America: Seeing Ourselves Through Our National Game. Washington, D.C.: National Geographic Society, 2002.

Enders, Eric. *Ballparks Then and Now.* San Diego: Thunder Bay Press, 2002.

Leventhal, Josh. *Take Me Out to the Ballpark: An Illustrated Tour of Baseball Parks Past and Present.* New York: Black Dog & Leventhal Publishers, 2000.

Lowry, Philip J. *Green Cathedrals: The Ultimate Celebration of all 271 Major League and Negro League Ballparks Past and Present.*
Reading, M.A.: Addison-Wesley Publishing Co., 1992.

Smith, Ron. *The Ballpark Book: A Journey Through the Fields of Baseball Magic.* New York: McGraw-Hill, 2002.

Ward, Geoffrey C. and Ken Burns. *Baseball: An Illustrated History.* New York: Alfred A. Knopf, 1994.

Atheneum Books for Young Readers
An imprint of Simon & Schuster
Children's Publishing Division
1230 Avenue of the Americas
New York, New York 10020
Copyright © 2005 by Lynn Curlee
Lyrics to "Take Me Out to the Ballgame" by Jack Norworth,
music by Albert von Tilzer, 1908.
All rights reserved, including the right of reproduction
in whole or in part in any form.
Book design by Abelardo Martínez
The text for this book is set in DeepdeneH.
The illustrations for this book are rendered in acrylic on canvas.
Jacket image description: A day at the ballpark
Title page image description: America's game
of summer at Wrigley Field

Mr. Curlee would like to thank Ed Peterson
for photographing the paintings.
Manufactured in China
First Edition
10 9 8 7 6 5 4 3 2 1
Library of Congress Cataloging-in-Publication Data
Curlee, Lynn.
Ballpark: the story of America's baseball fields /
Lynn Curlee.—1st ed.
p. cm.
ISBN 0-689-86742-5
1. Baseball fields—United States—History—Juvenile literature.
2. Stadiums—United States—History—Juvenile literature.
[1. Baseball fields. 2. Stadiums.] I. Title.
GV879.5.C87   2005
796.357'06'873—dc22   2003023144